SIGNS OF BEING

C.T. Perez

On the Cover

The cover of *Signs of Being* depicts a moonrise over the ocean with a cliffline in the distance and a small island visible at the horizon. A deep purple sky is sprinkled with constellations and the bright golden glare of the full moon, which breaks through heavy white clouds with light blue outlines. The celestial scene is sharply reflected in the water close to the horizon and then fades into the water's ripples, creating a softer effect where the book's title shines through. Moonlight pushes through the clouds, producing a space around the moon. This space and its reflection in the water faintly form the two parts of a latte, representing the foundation of ancient CHamoru homes.

Cover artist Jeffrey D. Harris painted the moonrise in soft and deep shades of blue and purple to capture the sense of calm he felt while reading *Signs of Being*. The heavy white clouds close to the horizon represent the chaos of colonialism and how much author C.T. Perez decries it. Like Perez's poetry, the clouds and the horizon are screaming in a quiet way. The moonrise and its reflection touch at the horizon like a high-pitched sound ringing in the ear, as though one universe is meeting the other, Harris described. Below the horizon, the water calms back down, returning to match the author's tranquil tone. The latte is meant to be subtle like Perez's work, Harris said. At first, it may not be seen, but once recognized, it cannot be disregarded.

PRAISE FOR *Signs of Being*

"In the Pacific literary firmament, long dominated by Polynesian (and select Melanesian) voices, C.T. Perez's *Signs of Being* blazes forth as a brilliant Micronesian star, demanding attention and reshaping our understanding of Oceanic literature ... Perez reminds us that in the vast constellation of Pacific stories, every island, no matter how small, shines with its own brilliance, contributing to the luminous tapestry of our shared human experience."

– **Selina Tusitala Marsh**, *ONZM, FRSNZ, New Zealand Poet Laureate 2017-19, and Professor of English and Drama, University of Auckland*

"Perez's sensuous writing invites us to explore and (re)imagine the mosaic of rich complexities that inform CHamoru histories, culture, language, relations, and contemporary experiences. Grounded in imagery, metaphor, and storytelling that is both refreshing and familiar to Låguas yan Gåni in particular and the Pacific more expansively, *Signs of Being* is a text of resonance, connecting the ocean and its people through shared realities and struggles."

–**Ha'åni Lucia Falo San Nicolas**, *2022 Indigenous Nations Poets Fellow and Doctoral Candidate in Indigenous Politics at the University of Hawai'i at Mānoa*

Signs of Being
C.T. Perez

University of Guam Press

PRESS

Copyright © 2024 by Cecilia C.T. Perez
All rights reserved.

Copyright is meant to respect the research, hard work, imagination, and artistry that go into bringing a publication to life. Please respect all copyright laws by not reproducing this resource in any manner without permission from the publisher except in brief quotations used for research, private studies, critical texts, or reviews.

University of Guam Press
Richard F. Taitano Micronesian Area Research Center (MARC)

303 University Drive, UOG Station
Mangilao, Guam 96923
(671) 735-2153/4
www.uogpress.com

ISBN-13 Hardcover: 978-1-935198-91-8
ISBN-13 Paperback: 978-1-935198-92-5
ISBN-13 Institutional E-Book: 978-1-935198-93-2
ISBN-13 Trade E-Book: 978-1-935198-94-9

Library of Congress Control Number: 2024941789

Editor: Verna Zafra-Kasala
Copy Editor: Vanessa Ochavillo
CHamoru Orthography Editor: Anna Marie Arceo

Cover Artist: Jeffrey D. Harris
Cover and Interior Layout Designer: Ralph Eurich Patacsil

This publication was made possible with support from an Equity in Verse grant from the Poetry Foundation. The Poetry Foundation recognizes the power of words to transform lives and works to amplify poetry and celebrate poets by fostering spaces for all to create, experience, and share poetry.

Note: The author has chosen to follow an older orthography in her spelling of "Chamoru." The word is now spelled "CHamoru" according to the official Guam orthography. Other instances of words that do not follow the official Guam orthography are also intentional and reflect the author's artistic choices.

Hu nå'i' gråsia yan hu onra
Ayu Siha I Manmaloffan Esta.

Dedicated in honor of
The Ones Who Walked Before.

TABLE OF CONTENTS

Hinasso – Reflection | 1
    Look at it This Way | **3**
    As I Turn the Pages | **6**
    Chamoru Renaissance | **9**
    Cut Green with Envy | **10**
    Bare-Breasted Woman | **11**

Finakmåta – Awakening | 13
    A Night at the Westin | **15**
    Kafe Mulinu | **19**
    Strange Surroundings | **22**
    Signs of Being—A Chamoru Spiritual Journey | **24**

I Fina'pos – Familiar Surroundings | 27
    Manåmko' Romance | **29**
    Invisible Ceremony | **30**
    View of Tumon Bay | **31**
    Saint Turtle | **34**
    Yoga Master | **38**

Lala'chok – Taking Root | 39
    Bokungo' | **41**
    Tatå-hu Bihu | **56**
    A Daughter's Goodbye | **58**
    Sky Cathedral | **60**

I Sinedda' – Finding Voice | 63
    Inside Out | **65**
    Tutuho' | **69**
    Of These Islands | **72**
    Banderan Guåhan | **75**
    Hand to the Sky | **77**

FOREWORD
Poetic Nonfiction at its Finest

Known to family and friends as Lee or Lila, C.T. Perez *(Familian Bino yan Familian Gollo)* shares with you, with her beloved island, and with our universe, this timeless collection of poetry and prose. These were produced largely as a part of her master's degree work in the Pacific Islands Studies Program at the University of Hawaiʻi at Mānoa. I first read most of these pieces nearly 30 years ago, some in gestational form, others finely polished. After graduation, life presented its numerous hurdles and challenges, and pieces of paper—even master's thesis projects—can sometimes fall off the radar. And so here we are, years later, reading this collection. Yet today, they provoke in me intellectual and emotional responses perhaps even more powerful than they did three decades ago. Such is the power of Lee's writing. Such is the power of what the Western world labels as "classics." In your hands, you have embraced a veritable masterpiece of Chamorro literature.

Lee and I serendipitously started the same graduate school program at the same time. We were casual acquaintances at that point, but history made us sisters. We took the same classes together, read the same books and articles, and engaged in the same discussions. And she never failed to stun me and our fellow classmates with her honesty and clarity. She had a remarkable ability to dissect complex issues and get to the core. But above all else, Lee always had the courage to speak up, even when knowing that her opinion, however truthful, might not be well received. Indeed, this volume of hers might not have been warmly received 30 years ago. So perhaps its long hibernation serves as a testament to the reality that it has taken the rest of us 30 years to catch up to her.

When we started our M.A. program in 1993, we continually heard the pained comment that Micronesia lacked a body of literature. Faculty members and graduate students alike pondered the silence of literary production from our islands. Lee and I, along with a fellow graduate student from Micronesia, the late Dr. Joakim "Jojo" Peter from Ettal in the Mortlock Islands, Chuuk, were frequently put on the spot to explain this lacuna. All kinds of speculation circulated. Could it be that our colonial overlords emphasized occupational disciplines such as agriculture and business, nursing and accounting, and pumped out technical reports, rather than fictional works? Or could it be that, as a people, we simply weren't inclined to express ourselves poetically? One scholar actually voiced a theory that perhaps there was an inherent pragmatism in the Micronesian mentalité that stifled the product of creative works (I'm not making this up). We pointed to the lack of local publication opportunities and wondered if the printing presses in our region simply struggled to keep afloat by producing textbooks and other financially profitable texts.

So, there we were in grad school, reading volumes of Pacific works by the likes of literary giants like Epeli Hau'ofa and Albert Wendt, Vincent Eri and Russell Soaba,

Patricia Grace and Witi Ihimaera. Long lists of Tongan, Samoan, Māori, Papua New Guinean, and other Oceanic writers populated our reading lists. Micronesia was stunningly silent. But today, the same cannot be said. Poet, scholar, professor, and writer-savant Craig Santos Perez *(Familian Gollo)* leads the charge not only with numerous publications, but also with national acclaim for his contributions.

The National Book Award in 2023 is only the latest, albeit the most prestigious, in a long string of accolades deservedly placed on Craig's shoulders. He had previously been recognized with the American Book Award (2015) and the PEN Center USA Literary Award for Poetry (2011). And Craig, as well published and recognized as he is, identifies Lee as "one of the most well-known and important contemporary writers from Guam."[1] He has written two papers focusing on the master's degree form of this publication, *Signs of Being*, referring to it as "one of the most important works of contemporary Chamorro poetry."[2]

Signs of Being tackles the major issues confronting Guam, perhaps even more intensely today than ever—colonialism, militarization, tourism, environmentalism, cultural identity, and urbanization, for starters. As Craig writes, "With all the changes that have occurred throughout the island's history, Perez hopes to wake up and recon-

---

[1] Craig Santos Perez, "Native Chamorro Ecopoetry in the Work of Cecilia CT Perez," *Ecopoetics and the Global Landscape: Critical Essays*, Ed. Isabel Sobral Campos. Rowman & Littlefield, 2018, 57.

[2] Craig Santos Perez, "Signs of Being: CHamoru poetry and the work of Cecilia C.T. Perez," *Jacket2*, 2011. http://jacket2.org/article/signs-being, 2.

nect to the land,"[3] and "implores CHamorus to listen to our ancestors struggling to speak through the silencing effects of colonialism."[4] Indeed, the voices and presence of our ancestors animate these works, as they continue to saturate our landscapes and culturescapes. For Lee, this publication represents more than a book of poetry and prose. Instead, its value lies in its use as a tool for decolonization, necessarily starting by breaking our minds out of the shackles of debilitating discourses that numb us to our Indigenous roots. Guam's history unifies her pieces, as she artfully addresses the lingering ill effects of Spanish contact and conquest beginning in the 1500s, Japanese occupation during World War II, massive U.S. militarization of the island after the War, and the postwar urbanization of Guam, including the growth of the tourist industry. For decades, my History of Guam students at the University of Guam have enjoyed "As I Turn the Pages," which appears in this collection. They go through it, line after line, appreciating the precise and vivid language that offers a damning critique of the mounds of research dedicated to the Chamorro homelands, only to invariably deny (albeit in sympathetic terms) our continued existence as a people. In this poem, Lee voices a resistant, emboldened cultural identity that speaks so clearly to the challenges facing all Pacific peoples as we confront the world's belittling views of who we are. So, yes, this is poetry, but it is also history. Yet Lee's history transcends the past. Rather, it links our past—our ancestors and the lands they died to protect—to

---

3 Craig Santos Perez, *Navigating CHamoru Poetry: Indigeneity, Aesthetics, and Decolonization.* The University of Arizona Press, 2021, 54.

4 Craig Santos Perez, "Signs of Being," 5.

our present condition and to our future challenges. The pen is Lee's sword, and *Signs of Being* calls upon each of us to deploy our unique gifts in the service of our people's strength and wellbeing.

Anne Perez Hattori, *Familian Titang*
Professor, History Program,
CHamoru Studies Program,
Micronesian Studies Program
University of Guam

Hinasso – Reflection

LOOK AT IT THIS WAY

When you're born
on an island

you
don't
know you're
on an island

until someone

tells you.

They ask,
"How can you
 live on such
 a sma-a-all
 island?"

I ask,
"How can you not?"

and,

"Sma-a-all, as compared
 to what?"

When you look at my island
what do you see?
Only a dot?
Barely a dot
on a map
point with your finger
or at least try
squint as you may,

you'll never find
or know
my island this way.

There is more to my island
than grayed cliffs
grassed hills
star sand beaches
edged by blue sea.

So vast is my island
it spans interwoven
through infinity.

Look into my eyes
brown dots,
my body the map.
See the shimmer of stars
having travelled from distances far?
Venture further in
you'll see where this island began.

From Brother Puntan
and Sister Fu'una
his body the land
his eyes the moon and the sun
from her energy
came life and sunlight.

My island flows
within me
currents surge

there is no delineation
of breath
from wind

of life waters
from seas.

My soul soars
unfettered,
Fu'una's light
emanating
eternal.

Did you call
my island
a dot
or not even a dot
on a map?
I say not.

My island is as big as the sky,
flowing to where
waves crest and fall.

My island reaches
beyond my breath
and from before all time.

In moon's ina[1]
and ma'lak[2] of sun
where my soul flies

my island lies.

---

1 Light.

2 Brightness.

AS I TURN THE PAGES

Hungry fingers
feed
searching eyes
rummage reams of text
between the lines
map the margins,
you'll never find
recordation
of Chamorro minds.

Translate
all you want,
archival
old Spanish
new English
some German, French, Russian, even
the rarely-talked-about Kanji.
You'll learn of flora and fauna
mountains
rivers
streams
and valleys,
that bêche-de-mer[1]
in Chamorro
is balåti'[2],
but
you'll never find recordation of Chamorro
thought.

In what has come to be called
"The History of Guam,"
severed from

---

[1] French term for sea cucumber.

[2] Sea cucumber.

sister homeland
Notte Mariånas[3],
the stage is set:
sleepy
colonial
island,
Nanyō[4], extension of Nippon[5],
and
bastion of American Democracy.

One of many scenes
is played:

foreign actors walk in
float in   fly in   bomb in
inseminate   into
the passive props.

Enter the props:
docile
indolent indios
tawny-skinned
muscle-bound
robust
thieving
ignorant
natives,
but...
they sail a great canoe!

I've read that script

---

[3] Commonwealth of the Northern Mariana Islands.

[4] Japanese term used to describe Japan's vision of incorporating the South Sea Islands into its national empire.

[5] Japanese term for Japan.

I've scanned those books
I've turned the pages
one   by   one
forward
backward
I've turned those pages
looking
sensing,
"Now, if those scholars,
learned men and women,
wrote,
'And in the end...'
'In one final gasp for life...'
'The last Chamorro died,'
then,
who am I
who know
my   self
to be Chamoru
and how is it
I sit here
thinking?"

CHAMORU RENAISSANCE

It's fashion
now
to claim
our roots
but yet
we cannot
face
we've stepped
across
a line
so thin
and shifted
to the other
side.

And though
we strain
to shape our
selves
exactly
to our past,
culture moves
like drifts of sand
and there is
no going back.

CUT GREEN WITH ENVY

While the rest of the known world
fantasized
and eroticized
life in the islands
among swaying palms
and balmy breezes,
I romanticized holding hands
in public
down crowded city streets
and exoticized linen-covered tables
set orderly with utensils
to frame
plates of meatloaf and gravy
buttered mashed potatoes
and cut green beans.

BARE-BREASTED WOMAN

For a moment
she had forgotten
where she was,
the daughter said
of her mother
who, earlier that morning,
had walked past convention
past the waiting cover-up shirt
into the garden,
into the light,
into the greens
and the feel of the breeze.

Her mother worked with breasts swaying
like her arms in color and swing.
There was grace in her stoop
and art in her till.
She worked, stooped, tilled
and planted,
even after
neighbors' gazes
called her
naked.

They could not see
that her skin
was their skin
richly drenched,
the color of earth.

The sight of her mother
squatting close to the ground,
too close to the color
of their own skin,

stripped them
and left them
standing naked
brown
as the day they were born.

Perhaps
they had forgotten
they were born
of this land
cured resplendent
by millennia of sun.

They must have forgotten,
the daughter was sure,
for as neighbors gazed
out pretty-picture windows,
a dark
bare-breasted woman
was all that they saw.

Finakmåta – Awakening

A NIGHT AT THE WESTIN

Strains of an old crooner song
persuade my brain
and seep into my senses

"Let's forget about tomorrow.
Let's forget about tomorrow,
for tomorrow never comes..."

And so I sit there at the Westin
poolside
listening to steel string guitars
playing
people laughing
I'm playing
I'm laughing, too.

The poolside is seaside
and I somehow know
not far away
lay my ancestors' remains
forgotten
by the builders of this Westin
who promised
integrity
dignity
and honored remembrance
in their re-placement
into new graves.

Scattered bones
invade my brain
seize my senses

cracked bones
my bones
burial desecrated.

Then
I'm crying
I'd forgotten, too
until I saw the plaque
metal cold
on the concrete railing
I struggle to recall.

As the evening cools
indigo into midnight blue
I expose myself
to the night-sown chill
that tries to steal
the last rays of sun
still warm within me
my hands move, cupped
fingers braided
to cover my head
with elders' voices
whispering all around me

adahi, adahi i sirenu[1]
I'm listening now
above the music straining
to chase the elders'
foreboding
away.

Fragranced balms
of night blooming jasmine

---

[1] Watch yourself, watch yourself against the night air

descend upon me
as if blown
like gentle kisses
so that the thought
of cracked bones
can evade my brain
and their healing mist
assuage my senses.

I hear the music
playing
people playing, laughing
as I look at smiles
I want to crack.

But I'm laughing
crying, too.

I'll write a poem
tomorrow
a letter to the editor
tomorrow
a short story
tomorrow
visit Their gravesite

tomorrow.

Content
with an icy piña colada
slushy sweet and smooth

Why did I have to look?
But once I did
I could not look away.

There was no music playing
early the next day
when we walked
along the beach
just below that happy place
we found the
grave marker
face down
and set it upright,

pull the vibes back
pull the vines back
inscient though they were
at least those vines gave their lives
to protect

your dignity
integrity
and honored remembrance

while all I did
was play and laugh and cry
and push thoughts of you
away until

tomorrow.

KAFE MULINU[1]

Taste bitter.
Taste sweet.
We sit
sipping
coddling cups
of brown liquid
and yawn in awakening
for the hour is late.
As we drink in
the brew,
our feet hesitate to rest
on what they know
too well
to be
concrete poured thick
over compacted wetlands.

Venetian-blinded windows
encase us in
conditioned air
conditioned minds
that keep us from seeing
keep us from feeling
the surrounding sessonyan[2].

Taotaomo'na,
our beloved ancestors
wail.
Cries from the past
whirl in the present

---

[1] Ground coffee.

[2] Wetlands.

are hurled at our presence
but only blow at us
like a whisper.

Our eyes perk
our heads tilt
as if to listen.
We are roused to remember
Their pain is our legacy.

We measure the weight
of our cup
grown heavy in our hands
that tremble with fear
at Their memories.

We leave Them in Their pain
as we heave
and take
yet another numbing sip.

Aii[3], mohon,   anggen siña ta hungok,
anggen siña ta nginge',
anggen siña ta li'e',

Mohon anggen siña ta siente
na ti åpman esta i ora,
siempre ti manmanmatåta'chong hit[4]
sipping

---

3 An expression of wistfulness or regret.

4 If only we could hear,
we could smell,
we could see,

If only we could feel
that the hour is late,
we probably wouldn't be sitting

coddling
cups of brew,
that keep us
dazed,
in open-eyed slumber,
thirsting for answers

that only leave us
still thirsting
heaving
groundless
sitting sipping
stirring mixing
tasting
bitterwithsweet.

STRANGE SURROUNDINGS

There is an unfamiliarity
of my surroundings
on my island home
where I was born,
where I have lived,
where I will die.

I look for a familiar tomorrow
elusive
escaping
just beyond my reach
tears well
reality penetrates
my skin
past my being
into my soul
that cries out
in morbid silence
before I am
no more.

I am lost in a wilderness
not of my making
drenched in my sorrow.

I seek The One Who Walks on Water
to help me rise above tide
past raging currents.

I seek The One
Who Walks on Water
to Pull me from this brackish waste
and Cloak me
in the finest wet air

of our deepest hålom tåno,
our deepest jungle,
to find the graces of
the Ones Who Walked Before.

SIGNS OF BEING—
A CHAMORU SPIRITUAL JOURNEY

I always come back to the idea of cultural survival. We are here. We are now. But what is it that brought us, as a people, to this point? Despite years of governance by colonial powers, our language and our ways persevere. We are not pickled, preserved, or frozen in time. We are not measurable or validated by blood quantum, ethnic breakdown, or physical characteristics. We are vital and vitalized by our tenacity and joined inner strength.

It is not in words spoken that we have been taught, but rather in the silent teachings of our *Saina*[1]. What we learn is to open ourselves to the collective memory of our People who came before us and help us to move ahead—i Taotaomo'na. They show us how to remain in spiritual love and connectedness with each other and our homelands.

Where do we go from here? We are in uncharted waters, or maybe in familiar waters, unable to recognize the signs that show the way. Am I a navigator? Am I *the* navigator? Are we moving? Are the islands moving?

With my diminishing eyesight, I try to expand my vision. I have stopped looking for signs and started feeling for signs. The islands are moving, and we are being guided. I felt my first wave, felt my first star, and felt my first island here in recent memory.

---

[1] Respected elders.

I was guided to Luta[2]. There, I was drenched in the tears and the sweat of reappearing, long-ago memories. I knelt in prayer in a field of felled Latte[3]. Steam rose from the earth in answer to the heat of the day and the blanket of rain that fell gently, straight down from Their eyes, straight down from Their sweating brows, pits, and loins. With my head bent low in homage, in humility and hurt, I breathed in what rose from the mingling of our tears and sweat. Somewhere between earth and sky, in the space where wind and sun merge, we were one.

The signs are before and around us, as friends and I witnessed in a quarry site for Latte. Some pillars lay above ground, cracked perhaps in the effort to move them. Other pillars lay still embedded below ground, along with some capstones. But it was not to these stones that I was drawn. I was compelled to walk to the corner of the field while my friends wandered in a different direction. As one of my friends noticed my interest in the single, slightly raised giant capstone and noisily approached, I stood. We went on to the other sites in Luta in true tourist fashion.

From then on, I was distracted, caught up in visions inspired by the Latte. A few days later, I returned with two friends. At first, the two wandered off as my other friends had days before. I started slowly toward the back corner again. My friend, Lina, soon joined me to warn me of the deep excavation I was nearing. "Did you see the capstone in that corner?" I asked. She said she hadn't, and I urged her to go to look. As she walked away, it began to rain.

---

2 Also Rota, one of the Northern Mariana Islands, visible from northern Guam.

3 Stone monoliths which indicate the strong presence of the Taotaomo'na, Chamoru ancestors. They are constructed with a vertical pillar that supports a bowl-like capstone.

I walked toward Lina, who I found kneeling before the capstone. The rain fell as quietly as I stepped. Lina did not notice me until I put my hand on her shoulder.

"Say what you're thinking," I said as I started to kneel beside her. "Tell Them what you're feeling. It's like praying."

Her body trembled as her words and tears broke through. "Guella yan Guello, håfa na ti en na'fonhåyan i che'cho'-miyu? What happened to make you leave your work?"

Her words struck me, and we held each other, embraced in Their spirit. We were touched by Their presence. Had They reached out for others who were trying too hard to see Them and could not feel Their presence? I wanted to give something of myself, an offering. I took a strand of my hair and laid it on the stone. I wanted Them to be able to find me again.

We have been walking together through space and time. The spirit of the People who came before is in us and surrounds us. It is in the call of the wind and the breath of our kiss. It permeates our psyche and fortifies our will to survive.

The fallen Latte is the sign. It is from within the row of Latte that we feel our strength. It is the severed capstone that gives us Their message, "Ti monhåyon i che'cho'." We will not rest until the Latte is whole.

I Fina'pos – Familiar Surroundings

MANÅMKO' ROMANCE

You chacha reggae
Unsure, I do the båtsu[1]
Our feet meet in step.

---

[1] A type of waltz popular in the early 1900s.

INVISIBLE CEREMONY

Strangers look
beyond the shores
of our island home
to find
color and pomp.

We don't need
Seekers of Truth
in search of the Noble Savage
to buy plane tickets
through
our home,
the "Gateway to Micronesia."

A turn to the left,
a turn to the right
will leave us
gasping
for air
in the exhaust of
hearts traveling
minds traveling
to find
notions of ceremony
they've only read of
in books while we, Che'lu[1],
disguise our selves
with our favorite costume
of dumb native
so we won't be late
to our ceremony,
invisible
only to their eyes.

---

[1] Sibling; used to describe or address a close friend or peer.

VIEW OF TUMON BAY
Circa 1996

Big hotels
skew the view,
and as if what we've got
ain't enough
Gov wants to build
MORE! MORE! MORE!

I thought selling yourself
was illegal
in this great Territory.

You say
two million by 2000?
I say
Oh, that's so too much!
I don't feel much like waving
I DO NOT
Welcome
All
Visitors
Enthusiastically

You WAVE, Gov
My hands are too busy
fanning away the stench
of tourist industrial waste
and praying for that
        threatened silence
if there were
no tourism
on Guam.

It's getting hard
to find a fish anywhere
except on a hotel dinner plate.

Two million
is just
too much.

Since when, nai[1]
was visitor
synonymous
with industry?

Tourism,
the ONLY industry?
That's a hard fish
to swallow.

Ombre lai[2], Gov
fanekungok put fabot[3],
it's not the ocean's roar
that's pounding in your ear,
can't you hear
the People cry

Diversify!
Diversify!
Diversify!

Maybe it's time to call
the legendary big fish bac

---

[1] An emphatic expression.

[2] C'mon man

[3] Please listen

to chomp Tumon
into the sea,
but you'd probably
just find a way
to sell that,
too.

SAINT TURTLE

I pray to you
Saint Turtle
and speak a tree
into being.
Cousins branch
but not of blood
so designed to be
of kin.

By the power of
the Holy One's shell
and promises of
Holy Eggs and Meat,
we join
in sacred silence
of our hidden harvest
from the sea.

Guella yan Guello[1]
once ate
turtle flesh,
once wore
turtle shell,
once drank
freely
the turtle yolk
of life.

The turtle
is a sacred meal.

---

[1] Reverent reference to Chamoru ancestors. "Guella yan Guello" is used in particular when directly addressing i Taotaomo'na.

It is holy
and sacred
that our lips
are wet with the juice
of life
that fed
the People
who gave
us life.

So, turn your head now
in disgust
if you cannot stomach this talk
of how a turtle tastes,
like something you never ate before
savory
soup
simmering
in the covered pot
in the back kitchen
under family's
watchful eye.

Each bite
of turtle
is taken
and treasured,
risking
penalty of law
foreign
to our
culinary ways.

Uncle says
he just wants
to eat

his turtle
in peace.

Throngs of people
gather
for Fiesta.
Biba!
Biba!
Biba!

Paper plates proliferate
piled high
with favorite food fare,
kelaguen uhang[2]
gollai åppan aga'[3]
pånglao[4] resurrected
into pehnot[5]
everyone
can eat,
sumptuous
but not sacred enough
to make
family of friend
with just one bite.

---

2 A savory dish made with mashed shrimp, onions, lemon juice, grated coconut, and red hot jungle peppers.

3 A starch dish made by boiling peeled plantains in coconut milk.

4 Land crab.

5 A complex dish, made with *pånglao*. It requires the captivity of dozens of *pånglao* for a couple of weeks during which time they are fed coconut meat. The crabs are then cleaned and cooked with må'son (a young stage of coconut), mint leaves, onions, and peppers. This mixture is stuffed into the body of the *pånglao*, secured with a decorative bow made of young sprouts of coconut leaves, and simmered in a pot of coconut milk.

Saint Turtle,
where is
Your Fiesta?

While we Saint you, Turtle,
they paint you turtle
Turtle
Turtle
swim in sea
U.S. law says
you are
free to be,
be tattooed
on the leg
of any native wannabe,
steal your spirit
take your soul
while
all we do
is eat
your gifts
of eggs
and meat.

YOGA MASTER

Through the open-air wooden slats
of my office windows
waves of island midday heat
break through
find me
eyelids drooping
eyeglasses
memos cast aside
I pinch my palms to stay awake,
it never works
I'm caught in the undertow.

Just past the languid flutter of my lashes
I spy my favorite boonie dog
drowsing
on his grassy yoga mat
posing into the downward dog
master of relaxation, he yawns
he is much smarter than me
he's found his shady spot
to stretch out and sleep.

Lala'chok – Taking Root

BOKUNGO'

The darkness of the cave tried to swallow the bright eyes of the child. Eyes of courage turned to tears as Lila's lips trembled and shoulders shivered in the cold dampness of the inner chambers of the cave. Her steps, bold and quick at first, had slowed. The tips of her toes worked as feelers over the edges of her well-worn *yore*[1]. She would have pushed her hands forward to help navigate herself through the abyss if she hadn't been so afraid of feeling the cave walls, slick and slimy against her bare arms.

From the dusty gravel road that ran under the San Ramon[2] cliffline, the entrance to the old World War II Japanese cave lay hidden, obscured and kept silent by the scars of shadow and light that the searing sun had slapped across its face. It was a stark scene, softened only by the gentle sound of children's laughter.

Up and over the short green grove of *tangantångan*[3] huddled a montage of children. They were siblings and friends, friends of *primos*[4], and *primos* of friends from the San Ramon neighborhood. They were gangs. Happy to be done with school and daily chores, they gathered. Their mouths puckered as they shared bags of salty seeds, *råk-*

---

[1] Rubber slippers.

[2] A district of Hagåtña village.

[3] Type of legume planted after World War II as part of a reforestation project.

[4] Cousins.

kio'[5], *daigo'*[6], and stories of recess-played games.

Like the cave's entrance, none of this could be seen from the road that ran by the children's homes. They were houses of wood and tin, Navy-learned masonry, thatch and planks, tarp and planks, and other building treasures salvaged from the rubble and surplus of post-World War II Guam and crafted into safe homes through Chamoru ingenuity and design.

Lila's house was the Bino house, home of her grandparents Tåtan Kiko and Nånan Chong Bino. Tåtan Kiko's *ramas*[7] was better known as Familian Bino, from the nickname of his father, Baldevino Taitano. This moniker distinguished them from numerous other Taitano family branches. Kiko was a nickname for Francisco, and so Lila's grandfather was called Tåtan Kiko Bino. His wife, Concepcion Castro Taitano, was known as Nånan Chong Bino, Chong being short for Concepcion. With affection and respect, the Bino grandchildren called them Tåta and Nåna.

The house was completely concrete, which was a big deal back then. It was strong against typhoon winds but altogether missing the gentle sound of rain against the thatched and tin roofs of their not-too-distant past. Just below the decorative masonry of the front porch lay Nåna's collection of pink, white, and red anthuriums—so perfect they appeared to be plastic. One step up and onto the porch was the obligatory screen door with its hand-

---

5 Pickled pearl onions.

6 Pickled Japanese radish.

7 Branch of a family.

made wooden frame, much sturdier than the mass-produced metal ones churned out these days. It closed with a "thud" and not a "slam" like the flimsy, nowadays ones.

Above the cliffline was holy ground, later called the Bishop's House. Namauleg Store marked the southeast entrance to their enclave, but of course, back then no one used words like "southeast" or "enclave." Places were called by the names of the families that dwelled there, a dedication to a beloved saint, a proliferation of particular trees or shrubs, or the prominence of distinct fragrances or odors. There were probably house numbers that the government required, but no one used them, no one knew them.

Of the San Ramon gangs, Lila was the youngest. She tagged along with her older brother Andy and older cousin Miget everywhere they went. None of them were allowed to go beyond the San Ramon street, so they spent their afternoons after school exploring the base of the cliffline. Some days they would play war with makeshift guns shaped out of scrap pieces of wood, rubber, and metal. Other days they would make slingshots out of tree branches and have target practice. Still other days they would dare each other to venture into one of the caves the Japanese dug into the cliffline.

San Ramon was Tåta and Nåna's home, where they loved and raised their children—the youngest being born just before the Japanese bombed and occupied their island. They knew the cliffline long before the Japanese gouged out its face, leaving deep gashes and open wounds. They called these caves "*bokungo'*," after the Japanese word for bomb shelter, *bōkūgō*. The *bokungo'* near their home was not only carved into the cliff but also deeply entrenched in Tåta and Nåna. The two *Saina*[8] never went near the cave.

Lila had lived most of her seven years in post-war, prayer-veiled Guam. She had entered the cave on a dare. It was a game the children of San Ramon played. Over the days and weeks, one by one the children would enter the cave. The test was to see who was not afraid, who could stay in the longest, and finally, who could go in the deepest. No flashlights, no lanterns, no sticks to use to feel around—those were the rules. Their goal was to become strong enough and brave enough to stay alive if there were ever another war.

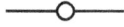

Since Lila was the youngest of the Bino kids who lived in San Ramon, she slept with Nåna. While the rest of the household settled into finishing homework and cleaning up after supper, Nåna and Lila would retire for the night. Rosary beads in hand, grandmother and granddaughter would pray their daily rosary while Nåna showed her catechumen how to hold the glass beads. Lila loved the rich gold-orange color of her diminutive rosary. The beads felt cool pressed between her small fingers, but mostly she loved her rosary because she felt she looked like Nåna when she prayed. After prayers, Nåna would let

---

8 Respected elders.

Lila blow out the Blessed candles. Throughout her life, the sweetly smoky smell this emanated would always remind Lila of praying with Nåna.

After prayers, Lila would stand on the bed behind Nåna and release Nåna's floor-length hair from its bun. She would comb it through, from roots to ends, with the *paineta*[9] that had held it in place throughout the day. Lila thought that when she was older, her mother would let her grow her pixie hair long so she could wear it in a bun like Nåna's. Lila added this to the list of things she would do when she was older.

As Nåna and Lila slept, soft evening breezes reached in through the slats of the glass louvers and screen to find Lila nestled in Nåna's arms. The young girl would try to synchronize their breathing. She liked the rhythmic rise and fall and the scent of Nåna's breath. Nåna smelled of clean laundry, coconut oil, Bengay, and Holy Water.

Startled out of sleep by Nåna's muffled cries, Lila would touch Nåna's face where tears should have been. Her little praying hands embraced Nåna's to assuage the elder's night worries and fears. Eyes wet with tears, Lila would drift off to sleep, her lips still moving in prayer.

When the first rays of sunlight broke one night, Lila asked Nåna what her dream had been about.

"*Cha'-mu hinalang, hagå-hu,*"[10] Nåna said. Then she tucked Lila into her arms and with her nose, pressed into her granddaughter's cheek in a loving kiss. She inhaled deeply, as if trying to take in the very essence of the child's innocence.

---

9 Spanish comb.

10 Literally, "Don't worry, my daughter."

"*Guifi ha'*,"[11] Nåna said.

Later, Lila asked her mother, "Why does Nåna cry when she's sleeping?"

"You're too young," Lila's mother said. "I'll tell you when you're older." She pulled her daughter into her arms and kissed the top of her head.

Determined to find an answer, Lila queried Andy and Miget: "Why?"

"She's thinking about the war," Andy said. "Before the Americans came, Nåna and Tåta almost starved. Sometimes they were beaten."

Again, she asked, "Why?"

"You're too young," Miget said. "Wait 'til you're older."

Now further into the cave than she had ever been, Lila wondered if this was what the darkness of Nåna's war dreams was like. Remembering how she comforted Nåna with her prayers, Lila found herself praying to chase away her own fears of being in the cave. Just ten more steps, she told herself, one for every Hail Mary. Starting at a whisper, her voice gained strength with each step.

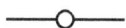

Outside, the neighborhood gangs spoke excitedly about the camp some of the older kids were building down the road and further up the cliffline. They were waiting for Lila to emerge from the cave so they could spy on the

---

[11] "It's just a dream."

campsite. There was still time before the sun hid behind the Cathedral's bell tower.

"How long has she been in there anyway?" Andy asked as he glanced at the sun dial he had made.

"She'll come running out crying any second now," Lila's cousin Bobby said. He had looped a rubber band through one of his *yore'*, trying to reattach the strap. He wiped the sweat off his brow and scooted toward the shifting shade.

"I don't know why we let her follow us," Miget said as he turned his attention back to the elaborate sketch of a heart with a girl's name in it that he had drawn into the dirt with a twig.

Her fears calmed by prayer, Lila moved further into the cave. A part of her brain that she could not control conjured up images of bats hanging upside-down, in droves, just over her head. She hoped none of these bats were related to the others she had seen swimming in a simmering pot of coconut milk and *dågu*[12]. Would these dangling furballs hold her complicit in the making of a dish that involved stewing the pungent whole bodies of what could have been cousins, siblings, or even parents?

Lila reassured herself with recollections of Andy telling her in his scientific, matter-of-fact way that Guam bats lived in trees. The poor girl believed her brother to be near-genius, and so, she could accept this tidbit as

---

12 Type of yam.

fact. She chanted this truth several times to ensure its authenticity.

"Guam bats live in trees. Guam bats live in trees. Guam bats live in trees," she enunciated in perfect textbook English, so as to add to the credibility of this statement. And for extra assurance, she added, "And I only ever ate the *dågu*."

Moments after her words disappeared into the ringing silence of the cave, Lila's brain was again busy screenwriting new images to frighten her. Complete and utter darkness had a way of illuminating dramatic and implausible realities in the mind of a child, yet on she went. She just had to stay a little bit longer and go in just a little bit deeper before she could turn around. *Almost, almost*, she thought to herself. *Just a bit more*.

Andy and Miget had shown her that if she spoke really loud into the cave, she would hear an echo come back.

"Hello!" Lila shouted, so very unlike her usual muted voice.

"Hello, hello, hello," in sequentially softening tones was the reply.

"My name is Lila!" she shouted.

"My name is Lila, Lila, Lila," the cave echoed back to her slowly, diminishing into a whisper.

Lila raised her eyebrows in amusement. It really did work. She could feel her body relax slightly.

She thought back to earlier that day. She had overheard Andy, Miget, and Bobby talk about exploring the cave. After school she was quick to change out of her

Cathedral Grade School uniform and put on her *bahåki*[13]. She then waited on the porch to make sure they could not leave without her. They tried to chase her back, but after they turned away, she quietly followed. By the time they noticed that she was still there, they were too far from the Bino house to send her back on her own.

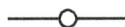

From her kitchen window, Nåna could see that the sun was getting ready to settle into Hagåtña Bay. Nåna, who knew the time by the cast of the afternoon shadows, was well into preparing the evening meal. During supper time, Nåna and Tåta sat down to eat only after all the children had eaten. More often than not, Nåna would eat from Lila's plate. Her granddaughter was a picky eater and left so much meat on the chicken bones. Nåna would eat the bones clean, gnaw on the *getmon*[14], and crack the bones to suck out the marrow. Nothing went to waste, not with her deeply rooted memories of wartime hunger.

Nåna glanced out the kitchen door to see her husband meticulously sectioning stalks of *tupu*[15] he had just cut from their yard. The children would be coming home soon to watch Tåta expertly at work with his pocketknife, peeling and cutting bite-size pieces for them to chew. While they ate, they would listen to his stories about places he had sailed to when he worked on a big ship. But

---

13 House clothes.

14 Cartilage.

15 Sugarcane.

at that moment, the house was quiet except for the sound of the blade against the tupu and the sizzling of onions in Nåna's pot.

Elongated shadows heralded the approach of supper time at the Bino house. Nåna stirred the butchered parts of chicken legs, necks, and wings. She had a row of quartered wedges of cabbage and potatoes all lined up to be added to the *kåddun månnok*[16]. She always added fresh corn to the pot just as the *kåddu* was done. As she added water to the pot, the sizzling stopped, and she noticed that she did not hear her grandchildren in the garage with Tåta.

Nåna was particularly aware that Lila was not in the yard. She worried about her youngest granddaughter because she was slight of frame and quick to cry. She called for Lila's older sister who was studying at the dining table which Tåta had built.

"Chana! Chana!" Nåna called.

Sissy jumped up when she heard Nåna call her by her Chamoru nickname. "*Ñora*[17], Nåna!" Sissy said as she pushed her schoolwork aside to run to Nåna. The rule was that when Nåna or Tåta called, the Bino grandchildren weren't allowed to ask, "What?" No, they had to be there at Nåna or Tåta's side within seconds, with the response "*Ñora*" or "*Ñot*[18]."

"*Hånao ya un espiha ayu na famagu'on. Esta*

---

[16] Chicken soup.

[17] A respectful response to the bidding of an older woman.

[18] A respectful response to the bidding of an older man.

atrasao,"[19] Nåna said.

Sissy was only two years older than Lila. Unlike her younger sister, Sissy always seemed to be doing the right thing. Sissy almost never got in trouble for anything she did. She had, however, gotten in trouble for mischief Lila had gotten herself into, so it was with great apprehension that Sissy set out in search of her little sister.

Shoulders slumped, Sissy headed for the door. At least she had an easy time finding her *yore'* on the porch since all the other kids weren't home. The screen door closed behind her with an ominous thud. The potential for punishment loomed. She wished she had kept a better eye on her younger sister, but then again Lila wasn't supposed to leave the yard without Sissy. She was annoyed because she had just showered and was getting dusty and sweaty walking up and down the dirt road that was their San Ramon street.

Sissy zigzagged around dried-out mud puddles and roadkill frog frisbees. She made her way up a short, steep incline, twisting through an entanglement of vines and brush as she trailed a narrow footpath to a campsite that the kids had started a few weeks earlier. She cross-stepped over piles of loose rocks and gravel and around tree stumps now thicker than a Coke bottle into the center of the kids' hideaway. Scavenged pieces of wood, tin, and burlap lay under the once-green camouflage of an assortment of twigs and transplanted weeds. No kids there. "Where is that little sister of mine?" Sissy asked herself with an exasperated sigh.

---

[19] "Go and look for those children. It's already late."

Lila must have sensed that enough time had gone by that she should start to make her way out of the cave. She had already bumped into the mossy walls twice as she moved deeper into the cave. She wondered if the walls were really as black as they looked to her now or if sunlight would reveal the true colors on her skin, shirt, and shorts. That was something she'd have to wait to find out. For now, she tried to guess how long she had already been in the cave. She held her breath, forgetting for a moment that although she could not see anything, she could still breathe.

Now deeper in the cave than Lila had ever been and full of bravada, she committed to five steps forward. Caught off guard by the sudden down slope, Lila's feet started to slide through her *yore'*, and she struggled to keep her balance. A chilled draft blew over her bare arms and legs. Even the smell of the cave changed, and the tips of her toes could feel an iciness to the cave floor. In a big *swhoosh*, a low howling wind bounced through the cave. Heart pounding, Lila did an immediate about-face, and in clumsy, awkward movements, she tried her best to run as she struggled to keep her *yore'* on her feet. Her arm brushed against the cave wall, and without a thought to its slimy feel, Lila used it to guide herself away from the howl and move rapidly toward what she hoped was the cave's entrance.

She thought she could hear Nåna's voice, and she kept moving toward the sound. Still stepping as quickly as she could along the wall, toes still gripping, cramped from trying to hold onto her *yore'*, Lila prayed, "Remember O Most Gracious Virgin Mary that never was it known that anyone who fled to your protection, implored your help, or sought your intercession was left unaided…"

Was that a glimmer of sunlight in the distance?

Pausing briefly to clean her glasses, Sissy had doubled back in front of the house, hoping to find the Bino kids had returned safely home. No luck there. As she passed by, she caught a glimpse of Tåta feeding the chickens at the back of the house. She moved quickly before Nåna would have a chance to see her. She could smell rice cooking, and it wouldn't be long now before Nåna focused her full attention on the whereabouts of her grandchildren.

Inside the house, upon hearing the rice water come to a boil, Nåna moved from cutting cucumbers to uncovering the rice pot and lowering the heat. She looked at the bounty of polished grain as they started to plump, and she Crossed herself and said a short prayer of thanks to the Blessed Sånta Marian Kåmalen[20]. Nåna prayed with gratitude that her family had plenty of food to eat. Through the window she could see her husband tossing feed to their free-roaming chickens and took note of a stalk of bananas almost ready to be picked from their small grove.

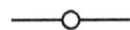

---

20 Patroness saint of Guam.

As Lila moved closer to where she thought the light was coming from, she didn't need to use the walls to guide herself anymore. Out of breath, her body heaved as if crying, but there were no tears. She was too scared to cry. Inside she felt like she was crying, but her eyes had no tears—just like Nåna. Were those voices she could hear? Finally straightening her body and picking her head up, she could see the arched outline of the mouth of the cave. She Crossed herself with relief.

Lila caught a glimpse of her arms, then her legs, now smeared with moss and dirt. She must have been hugging the wall as she rushed to escape the howling. She was so happy to finally see sunlight in the near distance. She took a moment to control her breathing. The animated voices of the San Ramon gangs grew louder. Lila stepped out of the cave and into the sunlight, shielding her eyes from its brightness.

Lila's calm demeanor elicited quiet amazement from the children. Then suddenly, a tall, shadowed silhouette appeared from a side trail, the sun casting a lit corona around its head and shoulders. All eyes shifted to the emerging figure. Once Lila adjusted to the newfound light, she saw with alarm that the tall figure was Sissy. Lila's eyebrows came together in a worried furrow.

Sissy cringed at the sight of her little sister muddied from head to toe with the red-orange colors the cave marked her with that she thought looked like dried blood. She nudged her glasses up with her nose and a backward tilt of her head. The younger one tried her best not to look at Sissy.

The neighborhood kids teased Lila, "*Toka, toka,*"[21] and "*Ma-gacha'*!"[22] Sissy gave them a stern look, and they stopped.

"Nåna's calling us home," Sissy told the other Bino kids. As Miget stepped forward, the Bino kids fell in line behind him and Andy.

One by one, the neighborhood kids started disappearing. They had Nånas and Tåtas of their own who were probably wondering why their grandchildren weren't home yet.

As they walked, Sissy waited for Lila's tears to come. The eyes of the young cave-stained girl were wide open now. She stood tall in the late afternoon shadows of the San Ramon cliffline. Her skin and clothing radiated in the late afternoon shadows that marked the day's passage. The corners of Lila's mouth maintained their brooding frown, but there were no tears to be seen. Sissy led her little sister gently by the shoulder and said in a soft tone, "Let's go home now." They walked together back to Nåna and Tåta and the Bino house.

---

[21] Phrase used to remind someone of impending punishment for a wrongdoing.

[22] Caught in a wrongful act.

TATÅ-HU BIHU

In faded khakis Tåta sits
Low Rider on his kåmyu[1]—
he's built it strong
of wood and steel,
persevering through the years.

Nåna asks for niyok[2] grated
as she creates our evening meal.
With his smile, a crescent moon relaxed,
after all-too-many years at sea
Tåta is more than happy to agree.

Too young to kåmyu on my own
I stand by Tåta's side
one of many lessons
only just begun
my job is to watch and learn.

With a *crack!*
coconut and machete meet back-to-back
and Tåta fills my glass.
The juice is sweet and smooth
but much-too-much for me.
Tåta drinks the other half—
in sync, we smack our lips and say, "ahhh!"
Tåta's taught me well.

At last!
The grating has begun,
and with ancient skill passed down

---

[1] Coconut grater.

[2] Mature coconut.

Tåta pinches the first sweet strands—
the treasure fills my hands,
then my face blows up like a puffer fish
as I try to chew it all at once.

Shoulders shaking, Tåta laughs
he's smiling down at me,
this, just one of many
days we shared
now cherished memories...
looking up I smile, too
at his loving, watchful crescent moon.

A DAUGHTER'S GOODBYE

Beads, beads
Holy beads
take me on their journey,
the color of my mother's eyes
brown wooden beads
finger-oil glistening
beads of sweat
beads at birth
beads at death.

I keep our days
like rosary beads
pressed tenderly
between my fingers
as I hold onto each one
for just a moment longer
but still
days
they slip away.

Cooing
rocking
I cradle my mother
in her last days
as she has cradled me
all through this womb of life.

Ordained,
I place Blessed Communion
into my mother's waiting hands.

In the night
I hear her praying
when she thinks that I am sleeping,

in silent murmurings I echo
listening
holding onto every word,
every breath
my tears
my fears confess
I realize
I might never hear my mother's voice
again.

Cooing
rocking
the fragrance of her
embraces me.

Intimate
meditative
the words flow sweet and sacred
like these last days
living, with a mother, dying—

I allow the beads to fall
into my loving hands,
so gently
I feel her breath, still
I close my eyes
and bow my head
one last kiss
This Holy Crucifix
against my lips.

SKY CATHEDRAL

Nåna lives
in jeweled nights,
stars like candles lit
in a sky cathedral
as she prays with angels
in the sound of wind,
she prays for me.

"Abe, Nånan Yu'os
Sen Gåsgas Maria
ma'-ogte minaolek
yan gråsia siha."[1]

Did you see that shadow pass
and pinch me on the cheek?
She misses me
and calls me from my sleep.
"Ñora[2], Nåna."
I whisper
with waiting watchful eyes.

I find her in gualåfon
full moon
dancing light
in a field of Latte
singing dreams to me,
gently then

---

[1] Lyrics from a church song that translates to:
"Hail, Mother of God,
Most Pure Mary
touches people
with goodness and grace."

[2] A respectful response to the bidding of an older woman.

she strokes my hair
with moonbeam fingers
lets each strand unfurl
and glisten in the wind
cascading to my shoulders bare
that greet this kiss
of Nåna's hair,
shining silver streams
that drape me with my past.

I am Nåna's daughter
born of earth and sky
scented breath
of salted breeze
surrounding seas
receive my soul
as Nåna takes my hands
to pray.

"Åbe, åbe,
åbe, Maria,
Åbe, åbe
åbe, Maria."[3]

Nåna lives
inside my poems
in the dusk-to-dawn of life,
Nåna lives in mornings
when I wake
before the light.

---

[3] Refrain for song, "Abe, Nånan Yu'os," which translates to:
"Hail, hail,
hail, Mary,
Hail, hail,
hail, Mary."

I Sinedda' – Finding Voice

INSIDE OUT
Circa mid-1990s

In the mid-1960s, I sat as a young girl in the back seat of my mother's car with my face pressed to the window. I squinted and focused my gaze on the car that sped along with us on a parallel road. We were separated only by a seemingly endless fence, which I could blur to nothing if I held my eyelids just so.

Across the fence lay another world on the same land, a world we called N.A.S., or Naval Air Station. N.A.S. was one of several U.S. military bases on Guam.

I was never able to follow the fence to see what it encompassed, but I learned quickly the lingo and feeling of exclusion it created. We needed a military identification card to go "inside." They didn't need anything to come "outside."

"Inside" lay spectacular cliffline views and expansive, well-manicured fields. "Outside," so I was repeatedly told, held nothing more than a distasteful quagmire of pothole-ridden, mud-lined roadways, indecipherable landmarks, nameless streets run rampant with wild dogs, and other remnants of what some would describe as an uncivilized world.

I knew that we were "outside" the luxuries of what was contained "inside" the fence. I had visions of the houses I could never see "outside." Theirs was an orderly world of tidy streets with neat lawns and clean sidewalks, all lined with evenly spaced, air-conditioned homes. At that time, we lived "outside," in a rented Quonset hut, marked by an inclined gravel roadway and a proliferation of *tåke' biha*[1].

"Inside," I had heard, kids were paid to do household chores that we did as just another part of helping family. I used to want what they had, or what I thought they had. As I entered my teenage years, I mimicked their style of dress and remember wanting a pair of faded blue jeans more than anything. I was ecstatic when, after my relentless nagging, my mom agreed that I could buy one pair of jeans. Her only prerequisite was that they be bought on sale at Town House.

I learned quickly that my success in life would be measured by how well I could emulate "inside" attributes and suppress "outside" characteristics.

The acquisition of the jeans was soon followed by the purchase of a puffer jacket that would have kept me warm in snowfall but should have been illegal in this tropical climate. These things could only be followed by my newly found desire for a Brady Bunch-inspired family room with a separate laundry room and dining room. It was a tall order for my single-parent mom of three teenaged children to fill with our typhoon-proof, compact, yet functional, Kaiser[2] home on a teacher's modest salary.

I'm sad to say that my mother died long before I learned to value my life "outside." I grew to adulthood accumulating the material wealth I associated with being from the "inside." I've long since surpassed the Sears catalogue ideal with a blend of *Architectural Digest*[3] and *This*

---

[1] A type of medicinal plant.

[2] Name of the first major subdivision housing development in Guam.

[3] High-gloss magazine featuring fine homes.

Old House[4]. A house, a condo, and some acquired land later, I've had my fill of trying to mirror the "inside." I have everything they had and more, and still, I find myself on the "outside."

Now, three decades later, I pass the same stretch of road by N.A.S. The fence still stands, although they say the base is phased out and the land has been returned. I manipulate my gaze to send that fence into oblivion once more, but when my eyes tire, the fence still stands.

When I first heard N.A.S. would be closed, I dreamt of how the fence would come down. I thought we could make a day of it. We would assign sections of the fence to different families to take down, accompanied by roadside barbecues and a freedom parade. Then I remembered the fuel line. Upon realizing that the fence was still needed to protect the pipeline, I altered my vision.

On the day of the closure, we should have had a million and one Guam flags tied to the fence. That would be a sight to behold. There was even an idea for a kite-flying picnic on that huge field by the main entrance or a caravan of cars through the grounds.

Then we heard. They weren't giving the land back.

The gates would still be maintained, but the color of the guards would change. They would put even more fences on their side to mark where they had dirtied our lands in perpetuity. They'll give the lands back, they said, when sufficient time has passed to prove we are competent caretakers.

Where the fence once made me feel wanting for the

---

[4] Public broadcasting television program on renovation of fine homes.

treasures I thought it contained, it now makes me feel the injustice for the stolen treasures it retains. I flashback to the man who scaled that fence in protest of the land being taken. He was apprehended and shackled by the military police. While others criticized his actions, I could only see him as brave. Restrained as he was by human force and metal handcuffs, he was free. He had freed himself in that moment from the psychological bondage of our colonial existence. In retaliation, he spit on his captor.

At first, I shuddered in disgust. "What low had this cultural hero sunken to?" I thought. After much reflection, my judgment changed. He showed bravery. What else could he have done?

Now, the landscape is changing. Whether you call it Tuyan or Tiyan[5], N.A.S. is gone forever. As former military homes are remade into GovGuam[6] offices; as the struggle continues between local government and private landowners; as the land tries to purge itself of negligent dumping; as motorists try to reclaim passage; as confusion reigns, the landscape is changing.

I've kept the blue jeans, worn in a style and meaning all my own. I've long since discarded the puffer jacket, having found no ornamental or functional use for it. I've given up trying to turn myself "inside" out. Now, years later, I can stand on either side of the fence. There is no "outside." There is no "inside." There is only what I allow to persist. The land is one. Today, the air smells sweeter, and the sun shines brighter. The landscape is changing.

---

5 In the renaming of N.A.S., traditional place names were suggested. The names Tuyan and Tiyan were the community's top choices and were different versions of the same Chamoru word meaning "stomach."

6 Government of Guam; Guam's territorial government.

TUTUHO'

Nanå-hu
Tatå-hu,
centuries pass
and still
I remember
I feel
war stories you lived
too painful to tell.

In your day,
you could not show weakness and live
Early graves claimed you
as they left you drowning in uncried tears.

Now, your pain lives within me

relentless
haunting
seizing me
with tears, sweat,
and the taste of your blood.

Tutuho' i lago'-hu
tutuho'[1]

Tutuho'
esta ki
tutuho' i masahalom-hu
tutuho'[2]

---

[1] My tears drip down
they drip

[2] Dripping
until
my sweat drips
dripping

Tutuho'
tutuho'
esta ki
tutuho'
tutuho' i hagå-hu[3]

Tutuho'
tutuho'
esta ki
kanna' måtai yu',
lao ti bai måtai.[4]

I cry blood
and drink tears
tears you could not.

Now, for you
I cry words
unbound
unfettered
unfurled
and hurled
they pounce.
På'gu'
ti bai dingu hamyu' Mañaina-hu
ti bai maleffa ni' manmaså'pet-miy
gi fehman i tiempon Gera...

---

3 Dripping
dripping
until
dripping
my blood drips

4 Dripping
dripping
until
it is as if I am almost dead
but I will not die.

yan i tiempon—
kinantidån såkkan—
despues.[5]

Bai na' mesngon yu'
bai fa'taotao yu' nu i irensiå-ta
sa' Tataotao-hu
Tataotao Hamyu'[6]

kada hu gimen i lago'-miyu
kada hu tanña' i haga'-miyu.[7]

---

5 Now
I will not leave you behind my respected elders
I will not forget your suffering
through the thick of the war...
and the time—
of all those years—
after.

6 I will make myself strong to withstand pain
I will stand strong in the humanity of our sovereign right
because my body/being
is your body/being

7 when I drink your tears
when I taste your blood.

OF THESE ISLANDS

I have risen from the ocean's depths
I stand strong on the reef's edge
bedazzled
salt crystals adorn me
I am here
I claim my place
Guåhan's daughter

of these islands
in these islands
I am born again
sun rays radiating
from within me.

I am of the people who have lived here
for thousands of years
and yet,
I am named for a saint
live on George Washington Drive
graduated from John F. Kennedy High School
and speak to you now
in English.

Miles away
the name game still plagued me
but in a previous colonial language.
Profesora from Cuba wants me to say
I am American
in Spanish,
but I cannot
I will not
because I am not

I say,
"Yo soy Chamorro."
She's flustered
I'm steadfast.
Our lands may be possessions
of an imperial power
but it does not possess me.

I stand strong
unyielding to
inculcation
acculturation
subjugation.

As a child I was forced to sing,
"Oh, beautiful for spacious skies,
for amber waves of grain . . ."

That's their song,
what's ours?

Cast into the chasm,
our voices halted
tainted
twisted
to these foreign tongues,
I cannot get their song out of my head.

Chamoru Warrior that I am
I have to think
dig deep,
fragments of songs and chants once known
permeate the air all around me
elusive, yet inviting me
to give voice to their spirit, rich essence,
and sing!

Tonight, in my dreams
I will hear your voices
where they've dwelled for millennia
living in my very DNA
I will gather our shards of song and chants
and make them whole
and I will fly like moonbeams
with abandon, I will gather your song
from this night symphony
of ocean waves and rhythms
hands raised to the starlit skies
untaint
untwist
my tongue
and sing
and sing
and sing,
your voices reigning!

BANDERAN GUÅHAN

Sing a song
sing a song to me
sing a song of liberty
sing of freedoms yet to be,
my country 'tis of thee
'tis of thee, Guåhan,
I sing!

Discordant myths
of history,
misperceptions of our reality,
these are the precepts
imposed on me.

Years of schooling,
scores of rulings
and still I think,
and still I stand,
and still I am a Chamoru
of these lands, these seas.

The tides of time are pulling apart
the seams
of Old Glory,
we were never counted
among their stars.

We wave our banner high
higher than the stars,
the mouth of the river
opens wide,
a chant
a charge
a battle cry,

Fanohge Chamoru!
Fanachu Chamoru!
Para i Manaihinekkog na tiempu Chamoru![1]

---

[1] Stand up, Chamoru people!
Stand strong, Chamoru people!
Forever Chamoru!

HAND TO THE SKY

Hand to the sky
the Ancient stood
feet bared in the cool depths of the sand
reaching
to measure the luminosity
of the stars
and the vastness of the skies.
Knowing
one day they would visit those stars
source of light
long after the sun had set beyond the horizon.

Pondering
the design
and engineering
of the stone foundations
that will one day
be called Latte.

I am
here in the meridian
in the twilight of time
of past and present
and what will be.

Kumeke pues tetteti uchan[1]
sheers of rain
blanket the waves
that salty mist
I taste the past
taking it in from around me
into me.

---

[1] It is as if it is about to rain, and then the first light drops begin to fall

I feel like an Ancient
as I stand here at water's edge
feet bared in the coolness of sand
as the rhythm of waves tries to carry me out to sea
—the pull is strong
to join the Ancients

but it is not yet my time.

The night sky is veiled with stars interlaced
each telling of an island that awaits
the bow of my sakman
upon its shores
so many stars
so many islands yet to see
the waves
the birds
the winds
beckon me.

I feel like an Ancient
as I stand here at life's edge
feet buried in the coolness of sand
the call of the Ancient tries to carry me out to sea
—the pull is strong

but I will not yet soar to that star
where Nåna and Tåta wait for me.

I gaze upon celestial brilliance
older than antiquity
in this meridian
this twilight of time
I revel in the knowing
that I am not the first star gazer
that I will not be the last

and the waves that are yet to come
will one day call me
Ancient.

ACKNOWLEDGMENTS

Thank you to the following publications in which these pieces, some in earlier forms, first appeared:

Galaide (Guam Communications Network, 1996) – "Signs of Being: A Chamoru Spiritual Journey"

Indigenous Women: The Right to a Voice (International Work Group for Indigenous Affairs, 1998) – "Inside Out"

Storyboard (University of Guam, Division of English and Applied Linguistics, 1998) – "Cut Green with Envy" and "Saint Turtle"

A Pacific Collection: Readings for Civic Reflection (Guam Humanities Council, 2011) – "Kafe Mulinu" and "Sky Cathedral"

Indigenous Literatures from Micronesia (University of Hawai'i Press, 2019) – "Bare-Breasted Woman" and "Look at it This Way"

AGRADESIMENTO

Signs of Being has taken a journey of almost 30 years to be published. It started as a collection of new poems, prose, and essays written for my Master of Arts degree in Pacific Islands Studies from the University of Hawaiʻi at Mānoa in 1997 and then was sent to bed in the university's Hamilton Library. Since then, parts of the collection have been given audience through course readers and a dedicated website, discussed in a number of online and print venues, and referenced in scholarly papers. On very rare occasions, I have shared my writing with close friends and family and at a handful of special events.

And then along came the very energetic, enthusiastic, encouraging, and talented fellow writer Victoria-Lola Leon Guerrero, who was politely persistent in her invitation to have *Signs* published through the University of Guam Press. I confess it was daunting to consider resurrecting a collection from decades past.

That invitation was the first step to having this collection published as you see it today. Heartfelt thanks to Lola, the director of the well-founded UOG Press, for seeing value in adding my manuscript to the Press' catalog.

Sincere gratitude and thanks to my editor, Verna Zafra-Kasala, for her generous, kind, and insightful creative direction in eliciting from me renewed and new poetry, and for her dedication to guiding me to become a better writer. Together we adventured through a sea of words to present this curated selection called *Signs*. We worked through the deeply personal, environmentally challenging, and life-changing effects and after-effects of that force of nature called Typhoon Mawar.

Warmest thanks to renowned international artist Jeffrey D. Harris, a longtime friend who graciously accepted the invitation to develop and design the cover art of this book, bringing with him his compelling perspective and distinctive brand of wit and talent, as well as his humility and generosity of time.

Thank you to the UOG Press staff for their unique and valuable contributions to present *Signs* in its best light.

Special thanks to the Poetry Foundation, whose generous support through their Equity in Verse grant afforded me the time, space, and resources for the publication of *Signs* to be realized.

Deepest thanks to the Dear Readers for opening the pages of this book and finding them worthy of their valuable time and attention. I am sincerely grateful to them and hope they enjoy the experience.

To my fellow travelers who have been with me on this journey of life and artistic expression, I bow down to fannginge', to kiss their hand in respect for sharing their knowledge, talent, and their treasured time. Ñot yan Ñora para esti siha:

Dr. Anne Perez Hattori, who never stopped believing that poetry and prose have a significant role in the teaching and telling of our history and who created and secured a space for such to thrive. My profound thanks to her for her lifelong dedication and commitment to elevating the discipline of Chamoru History worldwide. It touches my heart that a scholar of Anne's caliber sees value in my writing. I only recently learned from Lola that, for years,

Anne has been encouraging her to add *Signs* to the UOG Press catalog of publications. Anne is a true friend who has never stopped believing in me. I am forever grateful for our friendship, which has only grown closer through the decades.

Rudolph E. Villaverde, for showcasing my poetry and prose in the early days of the Internet, which gained an international audience for my writing through his web page. My utmost thanks to him for his lifelong friendship and for expanding my mind with our many conversations about history, historical perspective, science, and the stars.

Dr. Craig Santos Perez, who unearthed my unpublished manuscript from the Hamilton Library and shed his scholarly light onto my writing. My deep gratitude and appreciation for his vast achievements in literature and for bringing Chamoru literature to the world's attention.

Former U.S. Congressional Delegate for Guam and former University of Guam President Dr. Robert A. Underwood, Uncle Robert, for his phrase "as we move and groove through time and space," which set the direction of my poetry and prose in this collection.

Many thanks to the village of poets, writers, musicians, and scholars who in the mid-1990s gathered as friends to share and nurture creative endeavors and our dreams of building a body of Chamoru Literature: Si Difunto Frederick B. Quinene, Dr. Anne Perez Hattori, William L. Hernandez, Delores "Laling" Taitano Quinata, Lina Perez Taitingfong, Peter R. Onedera, Dr. Christine T. DeLisle, Dr. Vicente M. Diaz, and Dr. Keith Lujan Camacho.

As I worked through the writing of new poems and revising of older poems for this collection, I called on family to record themselves reading different versions of the same poems to help me finetune the flow and fluidity of verse. There was such beauty in hearing the poetry read by these sonorous voices. My profound appreciation is offered to them: Katherine Eclavea Taitano, Dr. Lilli Ann Perez, Alexandria "Sandy" Gould Yow, Susan Perez Kanehailua, Maria Perez Kanehailua, and Matthew F.T. Cruz.

For their gracious generosity in sharing their knowledge and experience of Chamoru culture and language, my forever gratitude is given to my aunts Si Difunta Clotilde "Diddy/Ding" Castro Gould and Si Difunta Jesusa "Ulang/Susie" Taitano Cruz, my Nina Isidora "Dora" Garrido Torres, and my cousin Theresa "Ewy/Saina Minetgot" Taitano.

Dear thanks to my niece Erin Malaca Retuyan who gave me the title to this collection and my Goddaughter Cara Christine Cruz for the power of her prayers which helped me to complete this collection.

To the late Dr. Robert "Bob" C. Kiste, founder and former director of the Center for Pacific Islands Studies, the late Dr. Karen M. Peacock, and Professor Emeritus Geoffrey M. White, my appreciation for allowing this creative writing approach to Pacific Islands studies.

With great honor and respect, I thank my grandparents Francisco Charfauros Taitano and Concepcion Castro Taitano "Bino," and Gregorio Flores Perez and Rosario Eclavea Perez "Gollo," for giving me a strong foundation in living Chamoru history through their life experiences and wisdom.

My mother, the late Teresita Taitano Perez, shared with me her love of words and books. We always had dictionaries, an abundance of books to read, crossword puzzles, Scrabble, and other word games in our home. Along with my brother, Andrew J. Perez, and sister, Susan Perez Kanehailua, we spent hours together reading or playing Scrabble into the night. My father, the late Licerio Eclavea Perez, passed on to me his love of visual imagery through his photography and the spoken word through his knowledge of making audio recordings. Words, books, imagery, and voice all gave rise to my love of poetry, for which I offer my loving thanks and gratitude to my parents, brother, and sister.

With fond remembrance, deepest thanks to my uncle, Si Difuntu Elias "Eling" Castro Taitano, for being the inspiration for my poem "Saint Turtle." He passed away shortly before the poem's publication and is greatly missed. May Uncle Eling now be able to eat his Turtle in Peace.

Lastly, yet foremost, to Gerard A. Cruz for his constancy and gentle, loving support and encouragement that gave me the confidence to complete this collection, I offer my dearest thanks.

Dångkolo na Si Yu'os Ma'åse' para todu esti na taotao siha. Tulos galaide', tulos, tulos!

Thank you for travelling through the pages of my life's journey. This collection started by taking pen to paper to write a simple phrase. One phrase followed another to become *Signs of Being*. I now invite you to write or draw your story into the following pages of this collection of thought, prayer, reflection, memory, vision, dreams, and fellowship. Si Yu'os Tenguan-mu!

C.T. Perez was raised in Guam. Her writing has appeared in *Indigenous Literatures from Micronesia* and *Indigenous Women: The Right to a Voice*, among other publications. She has an M.A. in Pacific Islands Studies from the University of Hawaiʻi at Mānoa and an M.Ed. in Vision Studies from the University of Massachusetts Boston.

www.ingramcontent.com/pod-product-compliance
Lightning Source LLC
Chambersburg PA
CBHW060534080526
44586CB00012B/725